THE JOY OF
HOLST

WISE PUBLICATIONS
part of The Music Sales Group

London / New York / Paris / Sydney / Copenhagen / Berlin / Hong Kong / Tokyo / Madrid

Published by
Wise Publications
14-15 Berners Street, London W1T 3LJ, UK.

Exclusive Distributors:
Music Sales Limited
Distribution Centre, Newmarket Road, Bury St. Edmunds, Suffolk IP33 3YB, UK.
Music Sales Corporation
Music Sales Corporation, 180 Madison Avenue, 24th Floor, New York NY 10016, USA.
Music Sales Pty Limited
Music Sales Pty., Units 3-4, 17 Willfox Street, Condell Park, NSW 2200, Australia.

Order No. AM1008821
ISBN: 978-1-78305-539-5

Edited by Sam Lung.
Arrangements by Andrew Skirrow and Sam Lung.
Music engraved and processed by Camden Music Services.
Cover designed by Tim Field.

Printed in the EU.

In The Bleak Midwinter

Gustav Holst

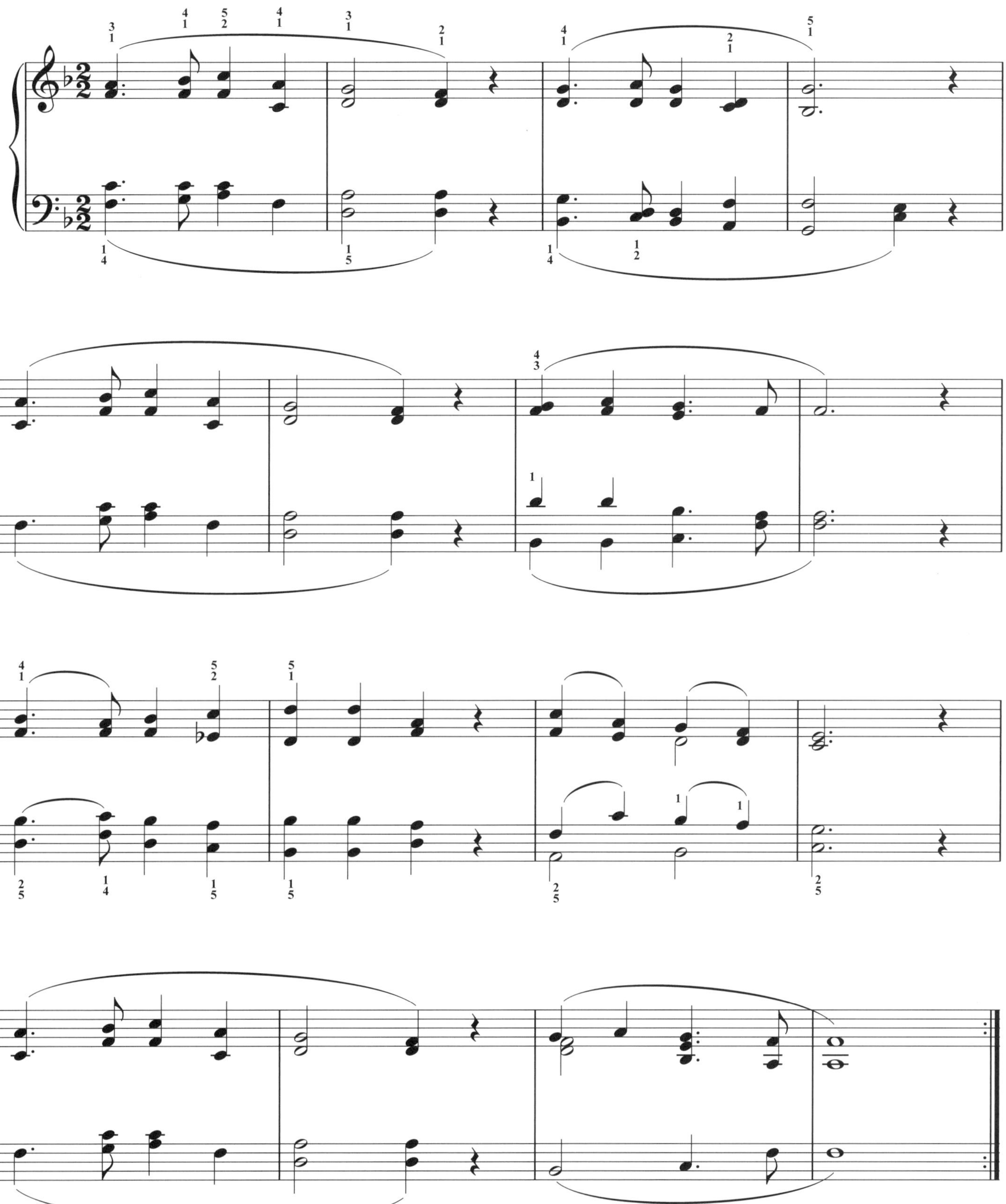

Jig

(1932)

Gustav Holst

cresc. poco a poco
8va

ff
dim.
p
f
p

cresc.
ff
dim.
p
dim.
pp
cresc.
f

cresc.
ff
f
sempre f

dim. poco a poco
p
8va
cresc. poco a poco

f
marcato
ff
meno mosso
rall.
p
senza misura
pp legato
ppp sub.
Ped.
Tempo I
ff

Nocturne

Gustav Holst

8va
f
cresc.
p subito
f
dim.
molto rall.
pp
Ped.
Tempo I
pp
8va
8va

8va
Animato
senza cresc.
f
sempre ff

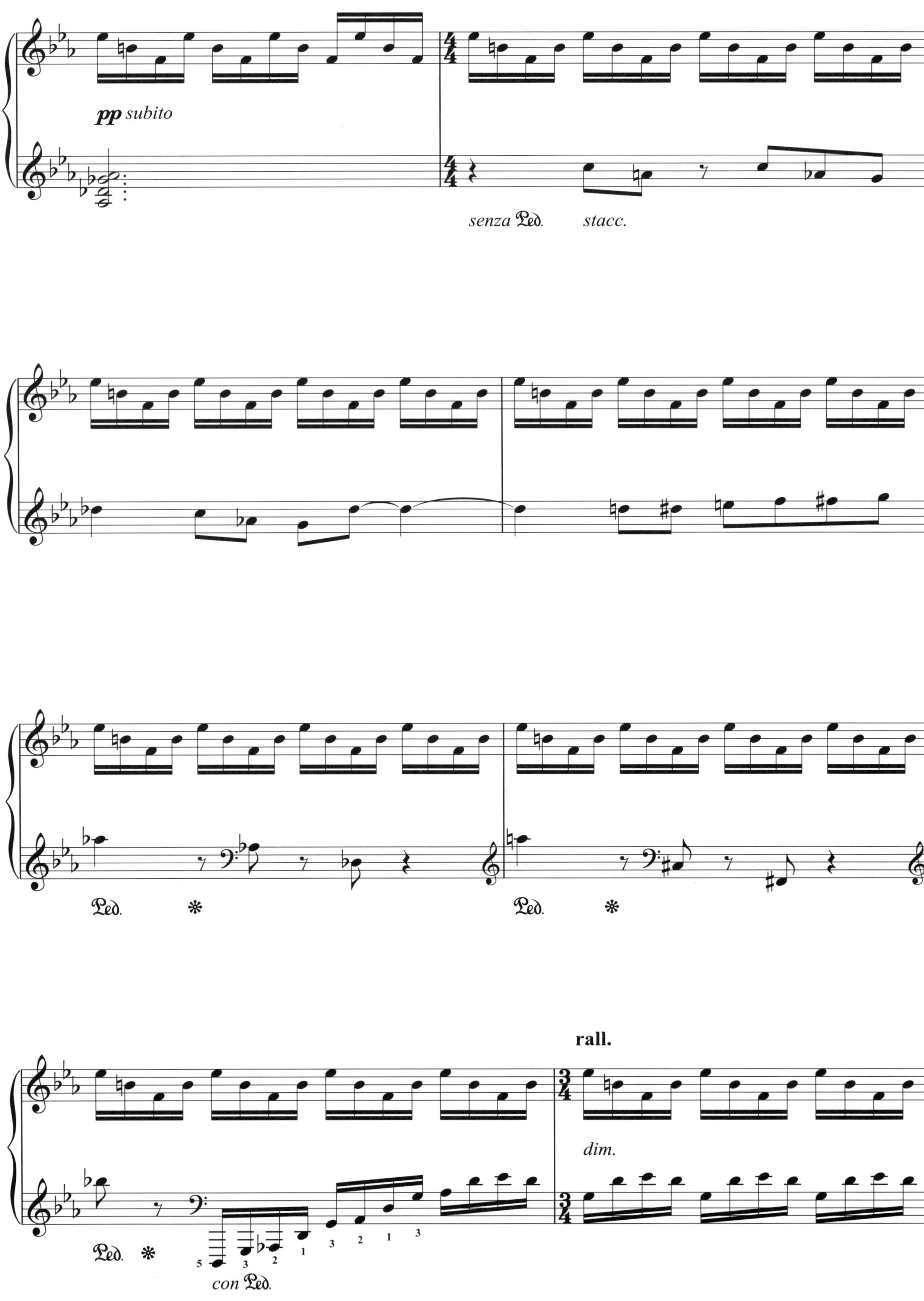
pp subito
senza Ped.
stacc.
Ped.
❋
Ped.
❋
rall.
dim.
Ped.
❋
con Ped.

Tempo I
8va
molto rall.
a tempo
cresc.
rall.
mf
p
dim.
Ped.

The Perfect Fool, Op.39

Dance of Spirits of Water

Gustav Holst

DANCE OF SPIRITS OF WATER

Allegretto

8va
(8)
p
mp
(m.d.)
(m.d.)
cresc.
mf
p

f
pp
8va
ppp sempre
(8)
(8)
(8)
(ppp)
(m.d.)
8va
(m.s.)
Ped.
*

Mars, the Bringer of War

No. 1 *from* The Planets, Op. 32

Gustav Holst

p
cresc.
mf cresc.
f
f cresc.

ff
cresc.
fff

ten.
ten.
ten.

ff
poco meno
f
sempre pesante
ten.
mf
f
ten.
mf
cresc.
f
f

f
mf
marc.
sim.
sim.
f cresc.

ff staccato
(𝅗𝅥 = 𝅗𝅥)
ff
p
cresc.

cresc.
8va
fff con fuoco
loco
fff

f
sim.
sim.
mf
f
mf
cresc.

cresc.
3
poco allargando

ffff
loco
ffff
fff
loco
A tempo
ff
mf
p cresc.
staccato
rall. al Fine
ffff
(ffff)

Venus, the Bringer of Peace

No.2 *from* The Planets, Op.32

Gustav Holst

p
p
pp
(m.d.)
Andante
mf
pp
una corda
p
tre corde

mf
p
Animato
mp cresc.
rall.
Meno mosso
f
pp
Ped.

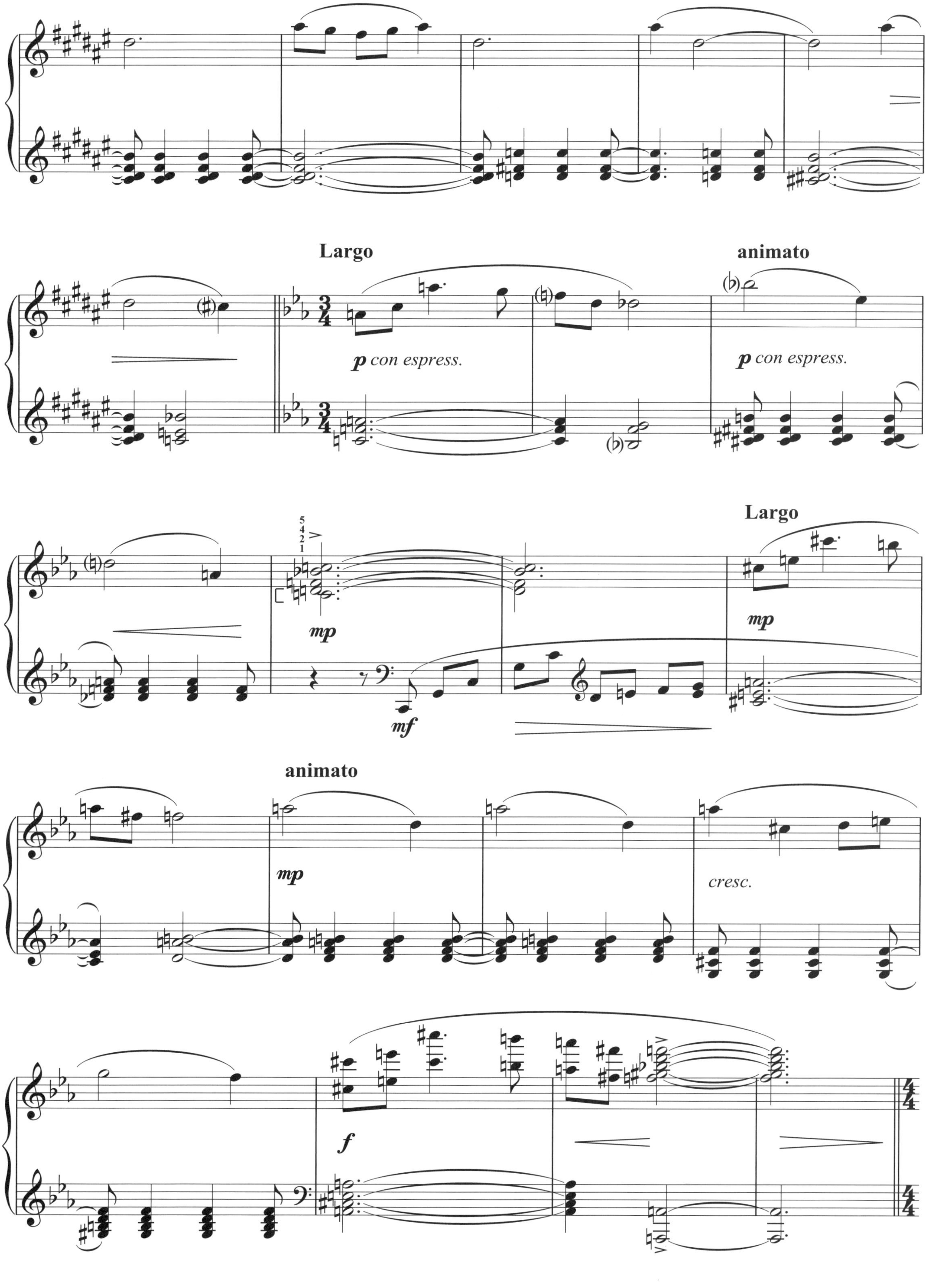
Largo
p con espress.
animato
p con espress.
mp
mf
Largo
mp
animato
mp
cresc.
f

Largo
Adagio (Tempo I)
p
pp
Ped.
8va
pp
(8)
Andante
mf

(8)
pp
una corda
(8)
p
espressivo morendo
ppp
Ped.
Tempo I
(ppp)
(p)
p
tre corde

pp
Ped.
legato
cresc.
dim.

8va
pp
una corda
legato
(8)
morendo
loco
8va
(8)

Jupiter , the Bringer of Jollity

No.4 *from* The Planets, Op.32

Gustav Holst

ff pesante

8va
mf
(8)
rit.
(accel. poco a poco)
f molto pesante (non legato)
sim.
mf
(a tempo)
8va
f
sim.

(8)
p
8va
5
3
2
1 1
p
cresc.
mp
(8)
f
f pesante
3
3
3

Stringendo
Più mosso
ff marcato

Tempo I
fff
dim.
mf
p
p
non legato

sempre p
8va
pp
trem.
Andante maestoso ♩ = 𝅗𝅥
pp
mf

f
ff

Tempo I
pp
pp
p
8va
pp
8va
(8)
loco
cresc. molto
mp poco marcato
Maestoso
fff staccato
Ped.
*

p
ff
f
ff
mf
f
f
mf
f

accel.
cresc.
f
marcato
Meno mosso
accel.
a tempo
f molto pesante non legato
7
7
mf
gliss.
8va
f
(8)
loco
mf
dim.
p poco marcato

p
poco marcato
8va
cresc.
f non legato

f
ff non legato
ff
p
cresc.

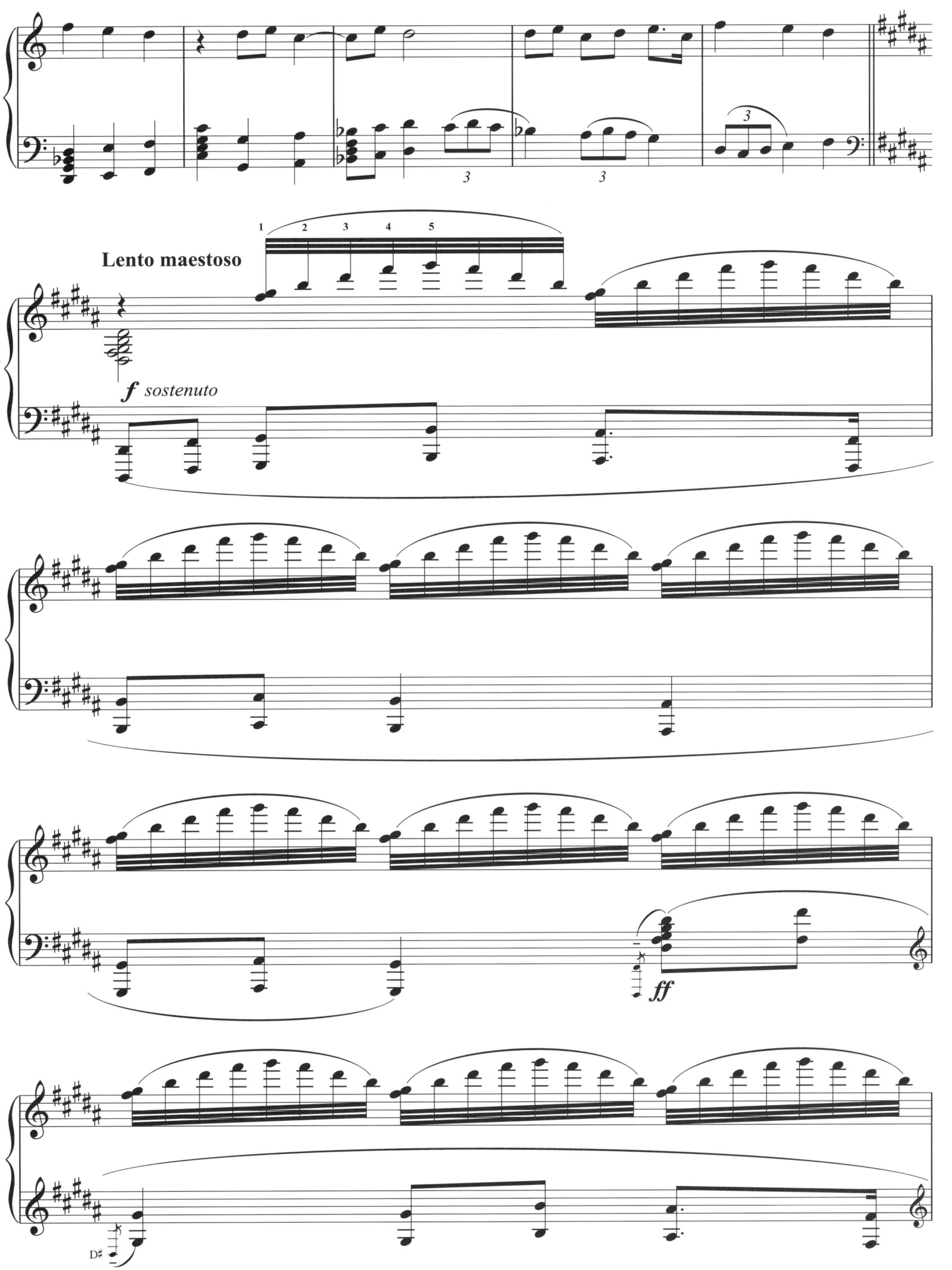
Lento maestoso
f sostenuto
ff
D♯

accel.
mf molto cresc.
Presto
fff non legato
sf

Saturn , the Bringer of Old Age

No.5 *from* The Planets, Op.32

Gustav Holst

p
Poco animato
pp
p stacc.
p ma sonore
p
3-4
meno p
cresc.

f
mf
pesante
dim.
Andante
ppp al fine
con Ped. al fine

(sempre ppp)
(sempre con Ped.)
(Ped. *)

A Somerset Rhapsody, Op.21

(excerpt)

Gustav Holst

(8)
pp
mf cresc.
(8)
A tempo
pp
f
(f)
pp
con Ped.
p
Poco
animato
p

Tempo I
mf
mf
(Ped. ❋)
cresc.
f
mf
(m.d.)
(m.s.)
pp
like distant trumpets
mp
pp
non legato
(quasi pizz.)
(pp)
(quasi pizz.)

p
(E)
(sempre quasi pizz.)
p
cresc.
mf
mf
mf non legato
pp

cresc.
forte

St Paul's Suite

I. Jig

Gustav Holst

ff
meno f
cresc.

ff
dim.
p
p non legato

cresc.
broadly

poco pesante
p
pp cresc. poco a poco
ff

pesante non legato
2
2
2
2
meno f

p cresc.
fff
sim.
molto pesante
non legato

Più mosso
ff
(optional)
(detached)
accel.
(stretto, in 1)
2
p
ff
2

Toccata on a Northumbrian Tune

Gustav Holst

p
mf

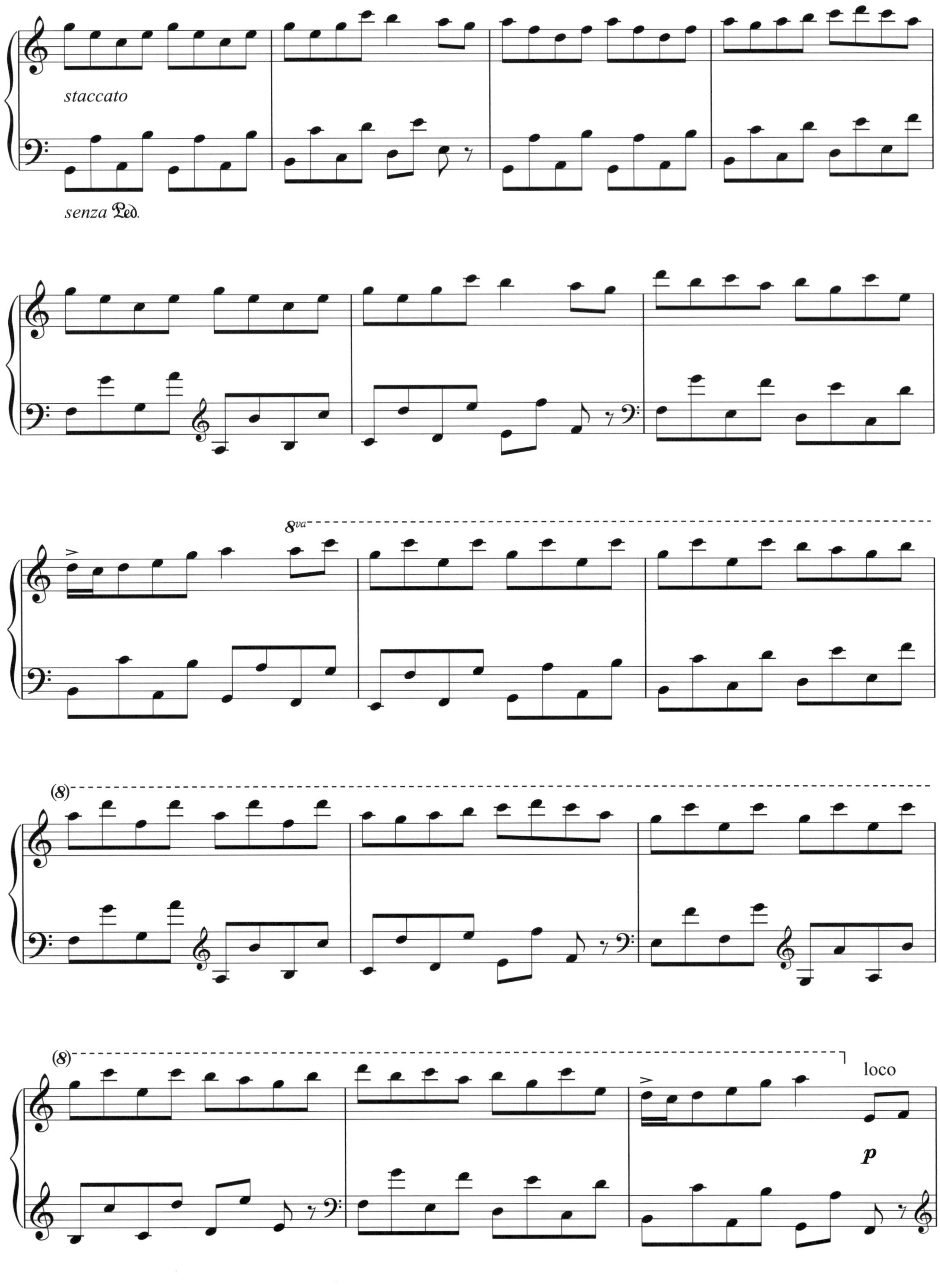
staccato
senza Ped.
8va
(8)
(8)
loco
p

p

cresc. poco a poco
f sempre cresc.
ff

* The *gliss.* should commence immediately *after* the G is struck; not *with* it.

8va
pp
una corda
(8)
(8)
(8)
poco cresc.
(8)
mp
tre corde

(8)
dim.
pp
8va

1 2 3 4 5 6 7 8 9